STEPS to RECOVERY

Emmanuel O. Afolabi

Copyright © 2016. All rights reserved.

No part of this publication may be reproduced, stored in a retrieval system or transmitted in any way by any means, electronic, mechanical, photocopy, recording or otherwise, without the prior permission of the author except as provided by USA copyright law.

All scripture quotations are taken from the King James Version (KJV & NKJV), of the Holy Bible, except where otherwise stated.

All characters appearing in this work are fictitious. Any resemblance to real persons, living or dead, is purely coincidental.

The opinions expressed by the author are not necessarily those of Revival Waves of Glory Books & Publishing.

Published by Revival Waves of Glory Books & Publishing
PO Box 596 | Litchfield, Illinois 62056 USA
www.revivalwavesofgloryministries.com

Revival Waves of Glory Books & Publishing is committed to excellence in the publishing industry.

Book design Copyright © 2016 by Revival Waves of Glory Books & Publishing. All rights reserved.

Published in the United States of America

Paperback: 978-1-68411-042-1

Table of Contents

FOREWORD 5
ACKNOWLEDGMENT 9
DEDICATION 10
PROLOGUE 11
INTRODUCTION 13
CHAPTER ONE
STEPS 1 & 2 DEVOTION AND AFFECTION 18
CHAPTER TWO
STEPS 3 & 4 REVELATION AND DETERMINATION 27
CHAPTER THREE
STEPS 5 & 6 INTEGRITY AND PERSISTENCE 36
CHAPTER FOUR
STEP 7 RESTORATION 42
ABOUT THE AUTHOR 49
Also Available By Emmanuel O. Afolabi 51

FOREWORD

The Author, in this book, "Steps to Recovery" shows the road map to recovery with assured, safe and secured success in Christ Jesus. One thing to note is that one cannot recover what one has not lost. Inclusive of lost but recoverable items are things stolen from us, either physical or spiritual; things are taken away from us by force usually by someone greater or stronger than one; or things which are carelessly thrown away by us. Another set of recoverable materials may include things we don't even know we have lost. Those things that rightly and divinely apportioned to us as heirs of the kingdom from the father of light belong to this category. Like the saying that except one discovers one cannot recover. In one's recovery road map, spirit of understanding and of wisdom must come into play and both are obtained from God. No wonder, the prayer of Apostle Paul for the Colossians Christians is very important and as well needful to us today in our steps to recovery. "So we have continued praying for you ever since we first heard about you. We ask God to give you a complete understanding of what he wants to do in your lives, and we ask Him to make you wise with spiritual wisdom." Colossians 1:9.

Apostle Paul equally prayed the same prayer for the Ephesians Christians, "I pray that your hearts will be flooded with light so that you can understand the wonderful future he has promised to those he called. I want you to realize what a rich and glorious inheritance he has given to his people." Ephesians 1:18. Both quotations are from the New Living Translation.

We need knowledge to discover, both of God and man that could lead to our discovery of lost items before the recovery of such by the power of God. The book presents a number of biblical images of recoveries with adequate descriptions in a single manner for better understanding of the readers.

For instance, Prophet Samuel's piece of information to Saul saved him from roaming about looking for his father's lost donkeys. "Now the donkey's of Kish, Saul's father, were lost. And Kish said to his son Saul, "Please take one of the servants with you, and arise, go and look for the donkeys." I Samuel 9:3 NKJV. Divine arrangements and connections are possible ways of God use for our recoveries. Saul sought for help and he was divinely connected with Samuel for divine solution towards the recovery of his father's donkeys. "But as for your donkeys that were lost three days ago, do not be anxious about them, for they have been found. And on whom is all the desire of Israel? Is it not on you and on your father's house?"

I Samuel 9:3, NKJV. Another biblical image of recovery presented in the book is that of David who recovered all, having lost materials and humans to the marauding Amalekites who raided, and burnt down Ziklag. "Then David and the people who were with him lifted up their voices and wept, until they had no more power to weep. Now David was greatly distressed, for the people spoke of stoning him, because the soul of all the people was grieved, every man for his sons and his daughters. But David strengthened himself in the LORD his God." I Samuel 30:4, 5 (NKJV).

The bible records it that David strengthened himself in the Lord his God in order to get comfort for his losses, information and direction from the omnipotent Himself for the way forward. "So David inquired of the LORD, saying, "Shall I pursue this troop? Shall I overtake them?" Hence, repositioning him for recovery expenditure that would be based on God's counsel, direction and instruction. And He answered him, "Pursue, for you shall surely overtake them and without fail recover all." So David went..." I Samuel 30:8, 9 NKJV. David according to God's declaration, RECOVERED ALL with spoils. The author gives assurance of recovery but only feasible through the power of God, in order to hasten and enhance your recoveries presented by the author are critical seven steps; devotion, affection, revelation, determination, integrity, persistence and restoration, Brother Emmanuel Afolabi is highly commended this effort in writing the book which I believe will uplift and encourage the body of Christ. Indeed the book has rekindled hope of recovery for as many who are going through the most difficult or dangerous aspect of ordeal or endeavor by way of loss of properties, loved ones, positions, jobs, faith, self-confidence et cetera. I therefore highly recommend the book to those seeking God's divine intervention for their various needed recoveries.

Revd. Dapo Longe

Senior Pastor/Zonal Superintendent

Foursquare Gospel Church in Nigeria

Jakande Zonal Headquarters Church

Jakande Estate, Isolo.

ACKNOWLEDGMENT

To God be the glory, great things he has done in helping me to accomplish the desire to put up this work.

I sincerely acknowledge the contribution of the Zonal Superintendent of Jakande Zone, Rev. Dapo Longe who wrote the foreword, for his interest in seeing that the project is a huge success, my beloved Associate Pastor Sola Adewale who I can refer to as my project supervisor and who wrote about the book. He indeed increases my enthusiasm, bolstered my moral and motivated me to work harder. My daughter Margaret Oreoluwa Afolabi who created most of her valuable time to edit the book.

I also appreciate the contribution of few friends who shown interest in this work.

It is my prayer that the Lord will bless them all in abundance.

DEDICATION

I dedicate this book to every reader that is going through one crisis or the other and to re-assure them that Jesus is the same yesterday, today and forever.

I have witnessed His mighty healing power for well over 20 years and also experienced His power to save and to deliver from every satanic attack. What he has done to others, He will also do for you.

As you read these Holy Spirit inspired book, believe that God is talking to you personally. Embrace every word and promise written therein and exercise your faith in them. As you marvel at what God did in the life of some of the characters in this book. Realize that God is not a respecter of persons.

Beloved, I dedicate this book to you, as you read through the pages; new things will spring forth within you that will bring changes and solutions to the circumstances surrounding you.

Blessed be the Holy Spirit that inspired me to bring this message of hope to you. My prayer is that as you read and meditate on the message of this book. God will reveal Himself to you a-new, and His overflowing blessings will fill your life and you will never remain the same again in Jesus Name.

PROLOGUE

The Holy Bible (NKJV)

The Bible contains the mind of God ,the state of man, the way of salvation, the doom of sinners, and the happiness of believers, its doctrines are holy, its precepts are bindings, its histories are true and its decisions are immutable. Read it to be wise, believe it to be safe, and practice it to be holy. It contains light to direct you, food to support you, and comfort to cheer you.

It is the traveler's map, the pilgrim's staff, the pilot's compass, the soldier's sword, and the Christian's charter. Here paradise is restored. Heaven opened, and the gates of hell disclosed.

CHRIST is its grand subject, our good the design, and the glory of God its end.

It should fill the memory, rule the heart, and guide the feet. Read it slowly, frequently, and prayerfully. It is a mine of wealth a paradise of story, and a river of pleasure. It is given you in life, will be opened at the judgment and be remembered forever. It involves the highest responsibility.

Will reward the greatest labor and will condemn all who triple with the sacred contents. Extracts from Gideon pocket Bible, the Holy Bible (NKJV, KJV) and quote from LIFE BIBLE STUDY and TEACHING MANUAL CHARACTER PART I Edition and Oxford Advance Learner's Dictionary 6th Edition.

INTRODUCTION

Recovery is defined by the Oxford Advanced Learner's Dictionary 6th Edition as regaining back something to its normal state or position after an unpleasant experience in time of trials or difficulty. It also means winning back a position, level or status that has been lost.

Proverb 23:18 states "For surely there is an end, and thine expectation shall not be cut off" which is the divine and authentic word of God for our lives. Expectation is the mother of manifestation; without expectation, there can be no manifestation. The book of Psalms further emphasized this point "Delight thyself also in the Lord and He shall give thee the desires of thine heart (Psa.37:4); our God is Real, Reliable and Dependable. "Behold I am the Lord, the God of all flesh, is there anything too hard for me?" (Jer. 32:27) He cannot fail. He honours His word more than His name; whatsoever He says, He will do. Therefore, your expectation in life shall not be cut-off; if you will dwell in the secret place of the most High, then you shall abide under the shadow of the Almighty, and there will be manifestation of your expectation in Jesus Name (amen).

In I Samuel 30, David and his men on returning from a botched attempt, at prevailing on King Achich to make him and his men to be part of his army to battle Israel (I Samuel 28:1-3; 29) found out that he and his men had lost all (i.e their wives, children and belongings). What could have been a relief for them (i.e their rejection from the Philistines army) turned into a monumental disaster, but in that state of deep sorrow and a possible revolt from his men (I Samuel 30:6).

David strengthened (i.e encouraged, in KJV) himself in the Lord his God. He enquired from God and God answered him (Psalm 65:2).

No matter how monumental the enemy portrayed your problem(s) to be, the RIGHT place to go is God. The enemy's strategy has always been "I will pursue, I will overtake, I will divide the spoil, my desire shall be satisfied on them. I will draw my sword, my hand shall destroy them" (Exodus 15:9) but through David's travail, we come to know God's antidote to the enemy's boastings/doings in your life, which is: Pursue (i.e do not give up-PERSISTENCE), for you shall surely overtake them without fail recover all" (I Samuel 30:8).

In the life of David and the lives of several others as will be revealed in this book, you will discover the steps to your recovery and as you apply the principles of the word of God to your own situation, you will surely recover for **"whatsoever things were written before were written for our learning, that we through the patience and the comfort of the scriptures, might have hope"** (Romans 15:4) **That which has been is what will be, That which is done is what will be done, And there is nothing new under the sun. Is there anything of which it, may be said, "see this is new? It has already been in ancient times before us".** (Ecclesiastes 1:9-10)

As you read this book, my prayer is that you will recover because your situations, circumstances, problems, troubles are not new, peculiar, that God will have to devise a new tool to tackle.

"So shall they fear the name

Of the LORD from the

West and His glory from

The rising of the sun.

When the enemy

Comes in like a flood,

The Spirit of the LORD

will lift up a standard

Against him"

Isaiah. 59:19

Rely on God and you will surely RECOVER.

Welcome on board on our voyage to the land of recovery. Shalom.

Emmanuel O. Afolabi

CHAPTER ONE
STEPS 1 & 2
DEVOTION AND AFFECTION

DEVOTION as defined by the Oxford Advanced Leaner's Dictionary (6th Edition) is showing great love, care and support for somebody or something. It also means prayers and other religion activities.

Job is an example of a man whose life is totally devoted to God as recorded in the Bible that he would rise early in the morning to converse with God for himself and his family (Job 1:5b) and this he did regularly facing each day in the presence of God. Job was totally devoted to God such that God Almighty Himself testified of Job as a blameless and upright man who fears Him and shun evil (Job1:8).

Job overcame his travails because he understood the importance of daily devotion unto God. God always makes Himself available to His people whether we see Him or not.

> "What is man, that You should Exalt him and that You Should set your heart on him? That You should visit him every morning, and test him Every moment? Job 7:17-18

David (the Psalmist) was another man who understood daily and early morning devotion to God (Ps. 88:13). He was a man totally sold out to God such that God testifying of him said "I have found David, the son of Jesse, a man after My own heart, who will do all My will" (Acts 13:22).

Therefore the first step to recovery in life is our devotion (i.e commitment) to God Almighty our Creator. For your expectation to come to pass as a child of God (i.e born-again, having accepted Jesus Christ as your personal Lord and saviour), you must give time to daily devotion (yourself and family) to God wherein lies strength to face each day under God's leading and direction.

When you are devoted to God. God will be devoted to your course in life. **For if you are known** to Him in times of your plenty, He will not abandon you when scarcity /adversity come.

AFFECTION as defined by the Oxford Advanced Learner's Dictionary (6th Edition) is a feeling of liking or loving somebody or something very much and caring about them.

The Bible commands us that we should love the Lord our God with all our hearts, our souls and minds (Deut:6:5, Matt. 22:37)

Your love for your maker should be unparalleled, for it is He who made us and not we ourselves, we are His people, and the sheep of His pasture (Ps. 100:3) He separated us from our mothers' wombs (Galatians 1:15) at the time appointed and thus deserves all our affection always. The person you love and whom you know loves you, you will have no restriction or reservation to go to in times of adversity for the Psalmist wrote "call upon Me in the day of trouble; I will deliver you and you shall glorify Me" (Ps.50:15). King Hezekiah is a perfect example of someone who demonstrated his love for God that the Bible recorded that he held fast to the Lord and did not depart from following Him, but kept His commandments, which the Lord commanded Moses (2 King 18:6). Thus, he was bold enough even at the point of death to present his scorecard to God concerning the message of God delivered through His prophet Isaiah.

"In those days Hezekiah was sick and near death. And Isaiah the prophet, the son of Amoz, went to him and said to him, "Thus says the LORD: "Set your house in order, for you shall die and not live'. Then Hezekiah turned his face toward the wall, and prayed to the LORD, and said, "Remember now, O LORD, I pray, how I have walked before You in truth and with a loyal heart, and have done what is good in Your sight." And Hezekiah wept bitterly. And the word of the Lord came to Isaiah, saying, "Go and tell Hezekiah, 'Thus says the LORD, the God of David your father: "I have heard your prayer, I have seen your tears, surely I will add to your days fifteen years," Isaiah 38:1-5

There is, however, a difference between loving God or loving the things that He provides or can provide for you i.e some love the things provided by Him, but their hearts is far from Him. GOD USERS NEVER WANTING TO BE OF USE TO HIM (John 6:24-26). Love is the embodiment of the covenant between God and mankind, for God demonstrates His own love towards us, in that, while we were still sinners, Christ died for us (Romans 5:8), and this is the reason why Jesus said the love of God and the love of our neighbor are the two commandments that the law and the prophets hanged on.

> "Teacher, which is the great Commandment in the law?"
> Jesus said to him, "You shall love the LORD your God with all your heart, and with all your soul, and with all your mind. This is the first and great Commandment. And the second is like it. "You shall love your neighbor as yourself. On these two commandments hang all the Law and the Prophets".
> Matt. 22:36-40

For your expectation to come to manifestation, you own it as a duty to love God and to love people. The person you love, you will not want to offend nor sacrifice to Him what cost you nothing. Job loved God (Job 1:1) and his love for God overflow to love for the people (Job 29:11-13) and in like manner David's love for God made him to refuse offering to God what cost him nothing (2 Samuel 24:24) and also refusing to accept from people what rightly belongs to God.

And David said with longing, "Oh that someone would give me a drink from the water of the well of Bethlehem, which is by the gate!" So the three mighty men broke through the camp of the Philistines drew water from the well of Bethlehem that was by the gate, and took it and brought it to David. Nevertheless he would not drink It, but poured it out to the LORD, And he said, Far be it from me, O LORD that I should do this! Is this not the blood of the men Who went in jeopardy of their lives?" Therefore he would not drink it.

These things were done by the

three mighty men"

2 Sam. 23:15-17

When your affection is towards God, there is no limit to what God can do on your behalf even if such has not occurred before, **for there is no precedent except God sets it.**

"And this is the sign to you from the LORD,

that the LORD will do this thing which

He has spoken: Behold, I will bring

the shadow on the sundial, which has gone

down with the sun on the sundial of Ahaz,

ten degrees backward. So the sun returned

ten degrees on the dial by which

it has gone down. Isaiah 38:7-8

"You have heard; See all this.

And will you not declare it?

I have made you hear new

things from this time, Even hidden things,

and you did not know them.

They are created now and not
from the beginning: And before
this day you have not heard them,
Lest you should say, 'of course
I knew them.'

Isaiah 48:6-7.

CHAPTER TWO
STEPS 3 & 4
REVELATION AND DETERMINATION

REVELATION

"... For there is nothing covered that will not be revealed, and hidden that will not be known (Matt. 10:26)

"... So David inquired of the Lord...and He answered him. "Pursue for you shall surely overtake them and without fail recover all" (I Samuel 30:8). Revelation is THE MIND OF GOD FOR ANY PARTICULAR SITUATION, but it is, however, saddening to note that when we are in difficulties, God is the last Person we consult, whereas really He should be our first. In the scripture above, until David inquired of the Lord, he has no clue as to what to do and if in his consciousness he felt pursuing them is the right thing to do, he does not know how that will turn out.

Until God speaks there is no solution to the jig-saw puzzle of our lives called "difficulties", hence we must learn to hear Him first before we make a move else we may end up on a wild-goose chase that produces nothing.

Success in life is a product of secrets and every successful venture has its trace to secrets and if you are a devoted and affectionate child of God, (John 5:20) His secrets are open up to you for "the secret of the Lord is with those who fear him" (Psalm 25:14) and "surely the LORD GOD does nothing unless He reveals His secret to His servants the prophets" (Amos 3:7).

How do you come about God's secret? For example through the prayer of inquiring like David did and through reading of His word as written in the Bible with the Holy Spirit bringing illumination into your heart. For you to know the mind of God for your life's situation you must be conversant with what He says in His word.

> **"This Book of the law shall not depart from your mouth, but you shall meditate in it day and night, that you may observe to do according to all that is written in it. For then you will make your way prosperous, and then you will have good success".**
>
> **Joshua 1:8**

God is God of principle and He will not bend or alter His word because of you rather you have to line up with what His word says and when you do what he says to you directly or through reading His word etc, your miracle is assured. David followed what the Lord God told him and he recovered all. For **"God is not a man, that He should lie, nor a son of man, that He should repent. Has He said, and will He not do? Or has He spoken, and will He not make it good? (Numbers 23:19).**

God surely makes good whatever he says.

"For as the rain comes down and the snow from heaven, And do not return there, But water the earth, And make it bring forth and bud. That it may give seed to the sower And bread to the eater. So shall My word be that goes forth from My mouth; It shalt not return to Me void, But it shall accomplish what I please, And it shall prosper in the thing For which I sent it."

Isaiah 55:10 & 11

Job was another man that learnt through pain and afflictions that there is no coming out of difficulties and challenges of life if God does not give direction. The counsel of men i.e (Eliphaz Bildad and Zophar (Job 2:11) and some of Job's belief about what he was passing through was not at all God's counsel, **"Then the Lord answered Job out of the whirlwind, and said: who is this who darkens counsel, by words without knowledge? Now prepare yourself like a man. I will question you, and you shall answer Me... And so it was, after the LORD had spoken these words to Job, that the LORD said to Eliphaz the Temanite, My wrath is aroused against you and your two friends, for you have not spoken of Me what is right, as my servant Job has"** (Job 38:1-3; 42:7). And when Job did according to the word of the LORD GOD, he got restoration. " Now therefore, take for yourself seven bulls and seven rams, go to My servant Job and offer up for yourselves a burnt offering; and My servant Job shall pray for you. For I will accept him, 'lest I deal with you according to your folly; because you have not spoken of Me what is right, as My servant Job has and the LORD restored Job's losses when he prayed for his friends, indeed the LORD gave Job twice as much as he had before' (Job 42:8 & 10).

With God, nothing will be impossible and to him who believe, all things are possible (Luke:1;37 & Mark 9:23). STOP relying on your know-how, stop depending on man; PUT YOUR TOTAL TRUST IN HIM WHO IS ABLE TO SAY AND TO DO.

> "Some trust in chariots, and some in horses; but we will remember the Name of the LORD our God.
> They are bowed down and fallen,
> But we have risen and stand upright"
> Psalm 20: 7&8

DETERMINATION

After God has revealed His mind to us on any situation we are passing through, we must be ready to act accordingly (i.e be determined to carry out what He says to you in spite of the difficulties it may entail)"... but Daniel purposed (i.e determined) in his heart that he would not defile himself with the portion of the kings delicacies, nor with the wine which he drank; therefore he requested of the chief of the eunuchs that he might not defile himself" (Daniel 1:8).

It takes courage to act in obedience to what God says especially against lives seeming gargantuan odds. However, note that you must make-up your mind to carry out God's instruction before you ask Him for His revelation, because it was not the time the table was set that Daniel made up his mind not to eat of the king's delicacies, it was before, else he will be distracted by the sweet odor and sumptuous look of what was set before him.

In like manner, God is not our mate nor a joker, so before you ask Him for His point of view regarding an issue, make-up your mind to do whatsoever He says.

Beloved nothing enhances your covenant blessing than faith and determination to trust Him absolutely (Jere.17:7&8): when you are embarking on a long journey or preparing for your examinations, determination is required in every endeavor in life, you need the determination to sail through,

"Though He slays me, yet will I trust in Him" (Job 13:15).

In time of distress, do you trust God or you trust in your own ability? Job was a man of determination. When things begin to fall apart around you, do you still keep your head afloat and determined to stay on the Lord's side? Will you say like Job that come what may, no matter what happens around you. I will not sin against God. That your business that is going down, unsettled bills that are mounting up and the financial crisis in your life have no other solution other than you determined to trust God who is able to bring to pass the desires of your heart.

You need determination to succeed. Your Christian journey requires determination, your sound relationship with God is the factor of your destiny fulfillment.

David was determined to do what God said which is "pursue" despite just returning from a long journey (I Samuel 30:10).

The story of the woman with the flow of blood for 12 years is a very good case study, of determination (Mark 5:25-28). She had undergone a lot of ordeals, physicians had subjected her to series of tests, she had spent all she had and it seemed the doctors in Israel at that time had finished all their prescriptions on her without solution. She became an object of ridicule within her vicinity, because of her prolonged illness, in fact the Bible said she had suffered many things from many physicians but instead of getting better, she was growing worse, but she was determined to get healed. She held fast to the word of God in Psalm 118:17

"I shall not die but live. And declare the work of the Lord".

Then a day came, she heard that Jesus the Great Physician was passing-by, and because she did not give up on herself making up her mind to see Jesus and touch His garment, because therein lies her healing. What a great faith indeed? What a determined spirit she has, she had to make a breakthrough to the large crowd that followed Jesus in order to touch His garment. Immediately, the fountain of blood dried up.

This woman had expectation that one day she would receive her healing and when the opportunity finally came, she grabbed it with both hands, and because of her determination in the midst of odds, she received her miracle. God is still the same, He never changes, He is no respecter of persons. He who healed that woman with the issue of blood is still alive, if you will only take a bold step today your miracle will come and you will have it in Jesus Name. God is able to bring you to your expected end.

CHAPTER THREE
STEPS 5 & 6
INTEGRITY AND PERSISTENCE

INTEGRITY

A man or a woman of integrity is one that is honest and upright in character at every material point in time. Circumstances and situations that occurred in the course of our lives do not change us, who we really are will show up under pressure.

> "And so it was, after the LORD had spoken these words to Job, that the Lord said to Eliphaz the Temanite, "My wrath is aroused against you and your two friends, for you have not spoken of Me what is right, as My servant Job has. Job 42:7

Your integrity must be visible to both man and God as Job, David and Daniel demonstrated. It was said of Daniel by his adversaries that no fault could be found in him except where they wanted him to violate the law of his God (Daniel 6:4&5). As for Job, his wife testified as to the integrity of her husband saying "Do you still hold fast to your integrity? " Curse God and die." In all this Job did not sin with his lips"; (Job 2:9&10) clearly revealing that a man of integrity is a man given to proper use of his tongue.

David demonstrated that he is a man of integrity before his followers and this he did in distress and in comfort. When Saul was pursuing him, first at it EnGedi in (I Sam 24:1-7) and secondly in the wilderness of Ziph in I Sam.26:1-12, David did all these in time of distress, no wonder when his followers saw the Egyptian lad in the field (I Sam 30:11), they brought him to David having learned of him regarding his treatment of Saul. David did not because of his predicament lose his integrity toward God and man. Even in the time of comfort, David remained the same in his integrity and a good reference to this was Abner. (for he was already king of Judah in (2 Sam. 2:11). Abner came to Hebron in 2 Sam. 3:12-22. David sent him away in peace.

Concerning these 3 men, God Almighty also testified. For Job, He said to Satan **"Have you considered My servant Job... And still he holds fast to his integrity..." (Job 2:3, 1:8 & 22).** The scripture record of God's testimony of David in Acts 13:22 **"I have found David the son of Jesse, a man after my** own heart, who will do all My will". For Daniel, the angel told him of the great love God had for him. Daniel 10:11.

> "And he said to me. "O Daniel man greatly beloved, understand the words that I speak to you, and stand upright, For I have now been sent to you." While he was speaking this word to me, I stood trembling" Daniel 10:11

Men of integrity stick with God come rain or sunshine, and their principles do not change under any circumstance for their slogan is **"I will not leave you till you bless me" (Genesis 32:26)" and though He slay me, yet will I trust Him (Job 13:15).** To men of integrity in good times, bad times, and at all times, God is God, and they are men who in spite of whatever is going on in their lives, they neither alter nor falter in their dealings with fellow men because their slogan will be "If you cannot beat them; STAND ALONE" not if you cannot beat them , JOIN THEM". With these men, women, boys and girls God goes all the way for them because He knew they are ready to go all the way to Him.

Psalm 50:23b "... And to him who orders his conduct aright. I will show the salvation of God".

PERSISTENCE

It is difficult to separate persistence from integrity as the two go hand-in-hand. Persistence is the consistency in doing or continuing or pursuing a course of action in spite of difficulties, even at the risk of being tagged annoying or unreasonable.

David, even at the risk of being called madman persisted in interceding for the child of Bathsheba conceived in sin(until he had whispers and concerning the death of the child) just in case, God will change His mind (2 Samuel 12:14-23). Paul said he pleaded with the Lord three (3) times that the torn in his flesh might depart from him, but God decides otherwise, hence he takes pleasures in infirmities... because God's grace covers all (2 Cor 12:7-10).

Persistent people also know when to call it quits as revealed in David's mentioned case. God's injunction to David in I Sam. 30 includes "Pursue" and to pursue requires persistence even at the risk of some of your kingdom partners becoming weary, you just have to continue because of what God said to you. (I Sam 30:8- 10&15-19) for PERSISTENCE ON THE RIGHT

PATH ALWAYS YEILD DIVIDEND i.e PERSISTENCE PAYS.

The story of Daniel in Daniel 10: 2 & 3, 12 & 13 is another example in persistence (in prayers),FOR THERE IS NO GIVING UP UNTIL YOU RECEIVE ANSWERS FROM THE THRONE OF GRACE, i.e until the day dawns and the morning star rises in your hearts.

> " And so we have the prophetic word confirmed,
>
> which you will do well to heed, as a light
>
> that shines in a dark place,
>
> until the day dawns and the morning
>
> Star rises in your hearts...."
>
> 2 Peter 1:19 .

Jesus, it is who told us of a widow and a judge in Luke 18:5-6 and in verse 7, He concludes by saying "And shall God not avenge His own elect who cry out day and night to Him, though He bears long with them? I tell you that He will avenge speedily..."

CHAPTER FOUR
STEP 7
RESTORATION

RESTORATION

Restoration (amongst the various definitions in the English Dictionary) is described as giving something that was lost or stolen back to somebody. This definition, however, comes short of God's kind of restoration because when God restores it comes in multiplication.

Restoration demands your believing and acting upon the word of God Almighty (i.e faith) for **"without faith, it is impossible to please God, for he who comes to God must believe that He is and that He is a rewarder of those who diligently seek Him". (Heb 11:6).**

One thing you MUST bear in mind always is that whenever you are passing through hard or tough times or difficulties as a true and worshiping child of God, you are still in the Porter's hands (i.e God). Even if it comes through sin, as long as you have cried to Him for forgiveness and you stick to God living out steps 1 to 6, God will restore you (Jeremiah 18:16). IF/WHEN SIN DE-FORMS YOU, GOD WILL /CAN RE-FORM YOU, only do not lose your faith (in God) and focus on Him, because the real issue is not whether God will SHOW UP, HE WILL; the real issues is that when He does, will He find you in place? (Luke 18:8).

> "For yet a little while, And he who is
> coming will come and
> will not tarry" Heb.10:37

When God gave David His word of recovery (I Sam.30:8) and he by faith acted upon that word, the Bible records in I Sam.30: 18 &19 "So David RECOVERED ALL that the Amalekites had carried away ... And NOTHING of theirs was lacking either small or great, sons or daughters, spoil or anything which they had taken from them; David RECOVERED ALL." Therefore faith and obedience hold the key to restoration, as well as not shutting up your bowels of mercy and goodness to people who needed it even in the midst of your trials and storms (e.g the Egyptian Lad, David helped - (I Sam. 30:11-16). David did not only recover their own possession, but also what the rampaging Amalekite soldiers took from other lands of the Philistines and Judah. (I Sam. 30:16).

Job likewise after his travails, in Job 42:9-12, the Bible records ...**for the LORD had accepted Job. And the LORD RESTORED Job's losses... Indeed the LORD gave Job twice as much as he had before... Now the LORD blessed the later days of Job more than his beginning...**" Here we see clearly that when God's restores, it is in multiplication and that for every devoted, affectionate, determined and persistent child of God who received God's revelations with the integrity of their hearts, things can only get better after every trial and storm of life, one key lesson to learn in Job's restoration was that he had to forgive his friends and then prayed for them, and it was only then God restored his losses.

"And the LORD restored Job's losses,

when he prayed for his

friends. Indeed the LORD

gave Job twice as much

as he had before"

Job 42:10

Finally, know this as a fact and do not forget it, **Restoration goes beyond human efforts,** for there are situations and circumstances that your efforts alone cannot tame or conquer, it takes GOD. With God on your side, you will always come out triumphantly, anytime and whenever trials and storms arise.

> "Now thanks be to God
> Who always leads us
> in triumph in
> Christ, and through
> us diffuses the
> fragrance of his
> knowledge
> in every place" 2 Cor. 2:14 .

Remember the following words and never doubt them.

1   **"Eye has not seen, nor ear heard, nor have entered into the heart of man the things which God has prepared for those who loved Him "I Cor. 2:9,**

" For since the beginning of the world. Men have not heard nor perceived by the ear, Nor has the eye seen any God besides You. Who acts for the one who waits for Him".
Isaiah 64:4.

" Oh, how great is your goodness, which You have laid up for those who fear You. Which You have prepared for those who trust in You . In the presence of the Sons of men!"
Psalm 31:19

2. "So, I will restore to you the years that the swarming locust has eaten, The crawling locust, The consuming locust, And the chewing locust, My great army which I sent among you." Joel 2:25

Nothing happens without God knows. Stick to Him and BE RESTORED IN JESUS NAME (AMEN).

Let's make this declaration:

1. I confess to God that I am a sinner and belief that the Lord Jesus Christ died for my sins on the cross and was raised for my justification. I do now receive and confess Him as my personal Lord and Saviour.

2. As you have therefore received Christ Jesus

    the Lord, so walk in Him, rooted and built up

    In Him and established in the faith, as you have

    Been taught, abounding in it with thanksgiving.

    Colossians 2:6&7.

    Assuredly you shall be restored.

    Shalom.

Emmanuel O. Afolabi

Tel: 0805-712-0673

0706-272-3037

0818-868-0576

Email:Emmanuelinterest05@yahoo.com

ABOUT THE AUTHOR

Emmanuel O. Afolabi has held several positions in many branches of Foursquare Gospel Churches in Nigeria since his salvation over two decades ago.

He has worked in the Christians Education Department where he was once the Discipleship Superintendent, Assistant General Sunday School Superintendent, for many years amongst others, at present, he is the General Sunday School Superintendent and Church Secretary of Foursquare Gospel Church, Ishoru Estate, Bucknor, Ejigbo, Lagos State.

He was formerly Purchasing Manager/Clearing Officer of Far-east Merchandise Company Ltd and Panalpina World Transport Nig. Ltd.

He is married and blessed with children to the glory of God.

Also Available By Emmanuel O. Afolabi

www.ingramcontent.com/pod-product-compliance
Lightning Source LLC
Chambersburg PA
CBHW050046080526
44586CB00014B/1478